First Facts®

Water in Our World

T0101236

Water Sources

by Rebecca Olien

CAPSTONE PRESS
a capstone imprint

First Facts are published by Capstone Press,
1710 Roe Crest Drive, North Mankato, Minnesota 56003
www.capstonepub.com

Copyright © 2016 by Capstone Press, a Capstone imprint. All rights reserved. No part of this publication may be reproduced in whole or in part, or stored in a retrieval system, or transmitted in any form or by any means, electronic, mechanical, photocopying, recording, or otherwise, without written permission of the publisher.

Library of Congress Cataloging-in-Publication Data
Olien, Rebecca, author.
  Water sources / by Rebecca Olien. — [New edition]
     pages cm. — (First facts. Water in our world)
  Summary: "A description of the Earth's water sources, salt water, and freshwater"—Provided by publisher.
  Audience: Ages 7-9
  Audience: K to grade 3
  Includes bibliographical references and index.
  ISBN 978-1-4914-8277-3 (library binding)
  ISBN 978-1-4914-8281-0 (paperback)
  ISBN 978-1-4914-8285-8 (eBook PDF)
  1. Water—Juvenile literature. 2. Water-supply—Juvenile literature. I. Title.
  GB662.3.O579 2016
  551.4—dc23
                    2015026113

Editorial Credits
Abby Colich, editor; Kyle Grenz, designer; Wanda Winch, media researcher; Laura Manthe, production specialist

Photo Credits
Capstone, 17; Getty Images: MCT/Quique Kierszenbaum, 9; iStockphoto: LynnSeeden, 19; Shutterstock: Christian De Araujo, cover, colores, 14, Ecelop, splash design, Lev Kropotv, 5, Matt Berger, 11, Mekt, 1, Mikhail Markovskiy, 20, niki_spasov, 7, Skibinski Przemyslaw, 12-13, tachyglossus, water design

Table of Contents

Water Covers the Earth

Earth is nicknamed "the blue planet." This is because water covers about 70 percent of Earth. Water fills oceans, lakes, and rivers. Water collects under the ground. Water is frozen in *glaciers*. Life on Earth depends on many sources of water.

glacier—a large sheet of frozen freshwater; glaciers are found in mountains and polar areas

4

5

Where Is Water Found?

Most of Earth's water is *salt water* found in oceans. Salt water makes up 97 percent of all water. Only 3 percent is *freshwater*.

Most freshwater is frozen in glaciers. Rivers and lakes hold a small amount of freshwater. The ground also stores some freshwater in *aquifers*.

salt water—water that is salty; salt water is found in oceans
freshwater—water that has little or no salt; most ponds, rivers, lakes, and streams have freshwater
aquifer—an underground lake

Oceans and Seas

Water found in oceans and seas is salty. It contains salt and other *minerals*. People can't drink salt water.

In some areas people have little freshwater to drink. They get drinking water from the ocean. They take out the salt so that the ocean water is safe to drink.

mineral—a material found in nature that is not an animal or a plant

8

Fact!

The salt in the ocean comes from rocks on land. Rain causes some rock to break down. Salt and other minerals from rock flow into the ocean.

a plant that removes salt from sea water

9

Water as Ice

Mountains and *polar* areas hold a small amount of Earth's water. Snow that falls in these areas does not melt. It packs together and turns into ice.

Packed ice and snow become glaciers. Glaciers cover large areas of land. Chunks of glacier ice break off into the ocean. They form icebergs.

polar—having to do with the icy regions around the North or South Pole

10

Fact!

Lake Vostok lies under a thick sheet of ice in Antarctica.

Lakes and Ponds

Freshwater collects in lakes and ponds. Lakes and ponds are sources of water for many animals. People drink water that comes from some lakes. Rain and snow add water to lakes. Rivers often flow into and out of lakes.

Fact!

Many lakes around the world were formed when glaciers melted.

13

14

Rivers and Streams

Rivers and streams carry water. Rain and melted snow flow into rivers as *runoff*. Water seeps into rivers and streams from the ground.

Rivers are important water sources. Animals drink freshwater from rivers. In some areas, the water people drink comes from rivers.

runoff—water that flows over land instead of soaking into the ground

15

Groundwater

Groundwater flows under the ground. *Precipitation* seeps into the ground. Water trickles down inside cracks and spaces in rock. Water then collects in underground aquifers. People drill wells to reach groundwater.

groundwater—water that is found underground
precipitation—water that falls from clouds to the
 Earth's surface in the form of rain, snow, sleet, or hail

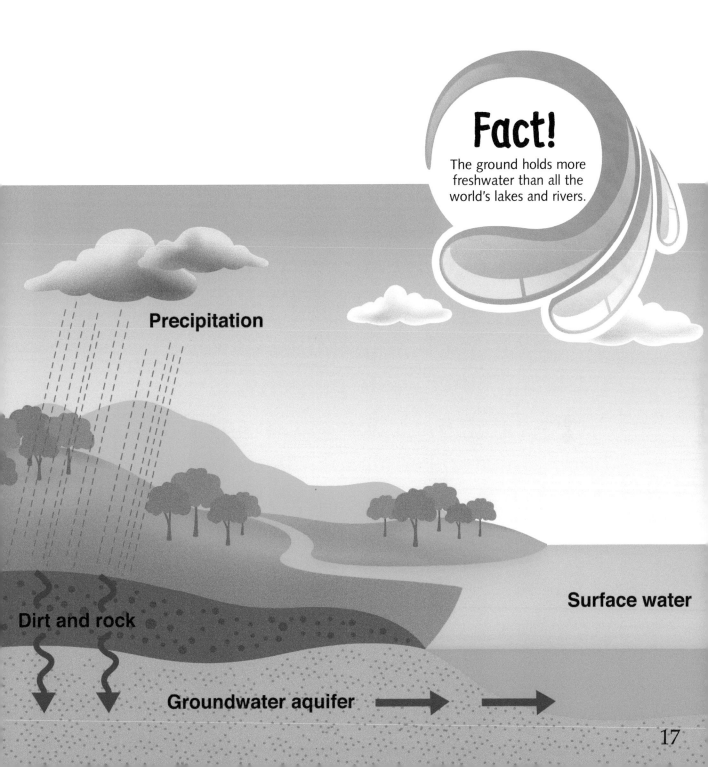

Fact!

The ground holds more freshwater than all the world's lakes and rivers.

Precipitation

Surface water

Dirt and rock

Groundwater aquifer

17

Protect Water Sources

Sources of water are everywhere. But they must be protected. Do your best not to waste water. Throw away trash and other waste properly. Never dump trash or waste in any body of water. People, plants, and animals depend on water from every water source.

Fact!

You can help save water by turning off the faucet when you brush your teeth. Taking shorter showers also saves water.

18

Amazing But True!

Lake Baikal in Russia holds at least 20 percent of all the fresh surface water in the world. It is the world's deepest lake. Lake Baikal holds as much freshwater as all of the U.S. Great Lakes combined. It is 5,315 feet (1,620 meters) deep.

Hands On: Groundwater

The ground holds more freshwater than all the lakes and rivers on Earth. Have an adult help you try this activity to see how water collects under the ground.

What You Need

- scissors
- clear plastic 2-liter bottle
- modeling clay
- 1 cup small rocks
- 1 cup gravel
- 1 cup sand
- 1 cup soil
- pin
- paper cup
- 1 cup (0.25 liter) water

What You Do

1. Ask an adult to help you cut the top off of the plastic bottle.
2. Flatten the clay on the bottom of the bottle about 1 inch high.
3. Layer the following items in the bottle, starting at the bottom: rocks, gravel, sand, and soil. These layers represent Earth's layers.
4. Use a pin to poke holes in the bottom of the paper cup.
5. Hold the cup over the plastic bottle.
6. Pour water in the cup. Let the drops of "rain" fall on the layers in the bottle.
7. Watch how the water flows through each layer and collects above the clay. Groundwater flows through Earth's layers in the same way.

Glossary

aquifer (AK-wuh-fuhr)—an underground lake

freshwater (FRESH-wah-tur)—water that has little or no salt; most ponds, rivers, lakes, and streams have freshwater

glacier (GLAY-shur)—a large sheet of frozen freshwater; glaciers are found in mountains and polar areas

groundwater (GROUND-wah-tur)—water that is found underground

mineral (MIN-ur-uhl)—a material found in nature that is not an animal or a plant

polar (POH-lur)—having to do with the icy regions around the North or South Pole

precipitation (pri-sip-i-TAY-shuhn)—water that falls from clouds to the Earth's surface in the form of rain, snow, sleet, or hail

runoff (RUHN-awf)—water that flows over land instead of soaking into the ground

salt water (SAWLT WAH-tur)—water that is salty; salt water is found in oceans

22

Read More

Ditchfield, Christin. *The Story Behind Water.* True Stories. Chicago: Heinemann, 2012.

Rustad, Martha E.H. *Water.* Little Scientists. North Mankato, Minn.: Capstone, 2014.

Spilsbury, Richard and Louise. *Oceans of the World.* Chicago: Heinemann, 2015.

Internet Sites

FactHound offers a safe, fun way to find Internet sites related to this book. All of the sites on FactHound have been researched by our staff.

Here's all you do:

Visit *www.facthound.com*

Type in this code: 9781491482773

Check out projects, games and lots more at
www.capstonekids.com

23

Critical Thinking Using the Common Core

1. List three freshwater sources on Earth. (Key Idea and Details)
2. What are the differences between freshwater and salt water? How do these differences affect humans? (Craft and Structure)
3. Page 6 states that most freshwater is frozen in glaciers. Page 10 discusses chunks of glaciers breaking off into the ocean. What would happen if all the glaciers melted into the ocean? How would this affect humans? (Integration of Knowledge and Ideas)

Index